WORDPOWER

(A 90 Day Devotional)

By: Joseph B. O. Pridgen
©2016

I dedicate this book to everyone who is thirsty for more of God. You always knew there was more. The POWER of God is waiting for you. Let's change the world!

-Joseph

DAY ONE

Read John 11:41-44

Check Your Connection

So I'm relaxing at the house and all of a sudden I get a text that says "call me back." I thought to myself, how can I call you *back* if we were never talking?

As if that wasn't weird enough, then I got a voicemail notification. But my phone never rang!!!! (Gotta love sprint) When I finally spoke to him, I found out that he called me twice, but my phone went "straight to voicemail". When I looked at my phone, the display indicated that I had 3 bars. But the truth was that I had no service.

What's the point?

Sometimes you can *look* like you're connected and *feel* like you're connected but not be connected to God.

So how do I know if I'm connected?

Simple. You make a call.

Are you hearing from God? If not, you might need to check your connection.

Pray with me:
Father I thank you for the privilege of prayer. Father if there is anything in my life keeping me from hearing your voice clearly and regularly, please expose it so I can remove it. In Jesus's Name, Amen.

DAY TWO

Read Matthew 6:11, 25-33.

Daily Bread

Do u know what the majority of our stress comes from? Worrying about tomorrow's bread.

How am I going to pay my bills next month? What can I do about my next payment that's coming up? What if something bad happens?

Do you know what Jesus' advice was? Don't worry about it. Enjoy today. Ask for what you need today. And be grateful when The Lord provides it.

The truth is that you're stressed right now; not because your "today" is in jeopardy, but because you're worried about being in trouble tomorrow.

Jesus said, as long as you have your "daily bread" then you're good. I took care of you today and I will take care of you tomorrow. Trust Me.

The only question is: do we trust Jesus...?

Pray with me:
Father, I know you take care of everything else, so you will take care of me. Even though I worry sometimes, help me to relax today and realize that you're in control... And you're good at it!
In Jesus's Name, Amen.

DAY THREE

Read Matthew 26:31-35, 40.

Check Engine Soon

Three of the most dreaded (and expensive) words in the English language are "Check engine soon"! I recently purchased a new vehicle and it automatically runs a diagnostic every time the cars turns on. Not too long after I bought the car, I turned the car on and saw te dreaded orange light that indiacted that my engine needed service. As soon as the light came on, the engine started sputtering and acting completely crazy! But the system had already warned me that there was something wrong with the car, so I took it to the shop immediately.

Jesus designed every human being with a similar system.

But do you know what I've discovered? Successful people aren't falling over themselves trying to give you advice.

Truly successful people are busy... Being successful.

But there are a lot of "critics with no credentials" out there who swear that they know how you should live your life.

That's why Psalms 1:1 warns us not to waste any time or energy on negative, ungodly people.

Because God knows that true wisdom doesn't just come from experience; true wisdom comes from God. "

Pray with me:
God, I thank you for every person that you have sent in my life to give me godly counsel. Father, increase Your voice in my life and curse every imitation that seeks to deceive me and lead me away from you. In Jesus's Name, Amen.

DAY FOUR

Read Exodus 3:1-6, 13-14

A Fresh Revelation

You need a fresh revelation of who God is. Whenever God is about to change the scene in your life, he always gives you a new revelation of who He is.

When God was about to elevate Moses from "shepherd" to "Deliverer/King" He gave him a new revelation of who He was.

*God knew that Moses wouldn't be able to handle his new assignment unless he could trust God on a new level. Stress and frustration come into our lives when we get elevated to a new level (with new problems) but don't have a new revelation of God. Because the "God" of your last situation may not be equipped to handle the problems that come with this new crisis. So you're stressed because you see problems you've never seen before and your revelation of God is too small to trust him in this new season.

So BEFORE you get elevated to a new level, God always gives you a fresh revelation of who He is, how powerful He is, what He wants you to do and how certain your success is in him. So the next time you find yourself in uncharted territory, with unprecedented danger, *relax*. God is just setting the stage so that he can show you a different side of Himself.
And elevation ALWAYS follows...

Pray with me:
Father I thank you for my elevation. I thank you for using pain to teach me that you are a comforter. Continue to show me your face and help me to fall deeper in love with you today. In Jesus's Name, Amen.

DAY FIVE

Read 2 Kings 6: 8-17

Open My Eyes

Did you actually read the scripture...?

The devotional won't make sense without it!

So, Elisha was surrounded by his enemies.
His servant was afraid and asked "What shall we do?"

Elisha responded, "Don't be afraid. Those who are with us are more than those who are with them."

The servant takes a quick count... "I see Me and Elisha... that makes TWO! How do we have more warriors than they do?!" His servant just didn't get it. So Elisha prayed "Lord OPEN HIS EYES" and the bible says that immediately his servant saw heavenly chariots of fire ready to help Elisha.

Revelation:
You've been praying for God to *solve* your problem.

Stop.

Instead ask God to open your eyes so that you can SEE the solution that He has already provided.

Pray with me:
Father, your word says that you have already given me everything that pertains to life and godliness. I thank you that you have already supplied all of my needs according to your riches in glory. Please open my eyes to see your provision in every area of my life. I pray this in Jesus's Name, Amen.

DAY SIX

Read Luke 4:18-19

The Power of Purpose

Do you know why you're here? If you don't know why you're here then I am willing to bet you that you are not walking in 1) Power 2) Passion or 3) God's Presence.

1. You're not waking in Power simply because "Power follows purpose". Jesus said, "The Spirit of The Lord is upon me and he has anointed me to..." The anointing ONLY comes to fulfill God's purpose for your life.
2. You're not living a passionate life because "Passion follows purpose". Most of us are always waiting for 5:00, or the weekend or a chemical substance to help us get excited. But if we were walking in purpose, Monday morning would be way more exciting than Friday afternoon. (yeah...let that sink in) If you're losing your passion in life it's because you're not walking in purpose. Jesus said, "the Spirit of The Lord is upon me! He has anointed me to preach GOOD NEWS". Jesus was excited about His message.
3. You're not experiencing the Presence of God like you know you can. Why? Because His Presence flows freely only in obedience to His purpose.
No matter how much you pray, fast, or "worship", you will never feel the fullness of God's presence as long as you're living outside of purpose. (Selah) There is a connection with God that you can't feel until you do what God does. Create what God creates. Fight what God fights. Your purpose is to "re-present" God in the earth.

Pray with me:
Father I thank you that you have created me for a purpose. Help me to find it and live it! Give me your power, passion and Presence as I fulfill your plan for my life today. In Jesus's Name, Amen.

DAY SEVEN

Read Psalms 8

Unplug

Facebook.

Instagram. Twitter. Snapchat. DM. Cable. Movies. Emails. Google. Yahoo. Text Messages. Phone calls. Business meetings. Radio. Cd's. iPods. Satellite radio. Pandora. Hulu. Netflix....

When do u have time to think?... Just think....?

The human brain needs down time. Time to recharge; refocus. Just like a computer, if you never "shut it down" you will permanently damage it. Our brains were not wired for constant stimulation. *And* if you're always plugged in to some sort of technology, when do you have time to hear God?
The Psalmist said, "when I consider the heavens..." He was sitting around one day and began to contemplate how awesome God was for being able to create the magnificent sky that we see.

When was the last time you were in awe of the sky? What about the stars? When was the last time you turned the tv off during a thunderstorm (like we used to do when we were kids) and just let yourself be immersed in the terrible Majesty of our God?

When was the last time you really unplugged?

Pray with me:
Father, I know you're always with me and I know that you desire to speak to me. Please God, help me to take the time to listen....
In Jesus's Name, Amen.

DAY EIGHT

Read Matthew 6: 1-6

My Instagram Life

One Mother's Day I went to Greensboro to be with my mom…and we took LOTS of pictures. I really enjoyed seeing my mom and my family and I wanted to capture those moments. Then I wanted to share those moments with the world...

I remember this one point in the afternoon when I actually made my family get up from the dinner table and go outside to take a picture. So that we could show the world that we were having a good time... at the dinner table...

While I don't believe that there's anything wrong with posting family pictures on social media, there are some people who try to post pictures to depict the phony happiness that they want people to THINK that they have. The Bible has a word for that: "Hypocrite".

I have actually seen people at functions FROWNING and NOT enjoying themselves right up until it's time for a "selfie" and then they smile like they're having the time of their lives...

So when you take a picture eating your lunch or going to the gym or visiting family or accomplishing some great feat, make sure that you're *actually* enjoying yourself and not just pretending for the camera...

Pray with me:
Father I thank you that you died so that I could really have joy and not just pretend to. Help me to walk in sincere joy today. In Jesus's Name. Amen.

DAY NINE

Read Luke 4:18-19, John 10:10

Anointed to Live

You hear the word "Anointing" thrown around in church a lot.

'Such and such' is so anointed. He's anointed to preach, she's anointed to sing, he's anointed to play, she's anointed to pray, etc... But why is it that when all these "anointed" people leave the church, their lives are still Jacked Up????

If Jesus really died on the cross, He didn't die just so I could sing well. If Jesus really shed His blood, he didn't shed it so that you could play an instrument and entertain. He died so that we could have LIFE! Abundant LIFE!!! After church is over, is anybody anointed to LIVE?

Is anybody anointed to laugh; anointed to care; anointed to succeed; anointed to actually help others?

Or did Jesus die just so we could be good at "church"...?

Pray with me:
Jesus I thank you for dying so that I could live. Your blood bought me abundant life and I repent for every second that I lived in bondage and defeat. You said that you were the resurrection and the life; Teach me how to live. Really live. In Jesus's Name, Amen.

DAY TEN

Read 2 Corinthians 10:4-5

Strongholds

I love Walmart, but I always wind up spending too much money when I go! So the other day I decided to make a list and ONLY take enough money to buy the things on my list. But when I got to Walmart they had one of my items in sale "Buy one get one free!!!" (Now this is a $20.00 item.)

Immediately I got upset. "See this is why I never do this! If I had brought more money I could have saved more money! I buy this product every month! Every package I buy is saving me $20.00!!!! I want to buy 2 or 3!!!!"

So I texted my wife and told her the "bad news" about not taking a lot of money and the product being on a "BOGO" sale. Do you know what her response was?

"Praise The Lord!"

It wasn't until that moment that I realized that instead of being upset that I couldn't buy multiple packs; I should have been praising God that he DOUBLED my money's value at Walmart! Point: How many miracles have you missed because you had the wrong point of view....? That's a Stronghold.

Pray with me:
Father, please open my eyes to see the answers to my prayers when you send them. And help me to be grateful. In Jesus's Name, Amen.

DAY ELEVEN

Joshua 1:5-9

Overcoming the Spirit of Fear

Hear this Word from God: <u>There is nothing standing between you and your destiny but the faith to believe it will happen.</u> The gift of God is already inside you. All you have to do is stir it up and the Word promises that your gift will make room for you. (2 Timothy 1:6, Proverbs 18:16)
The Word of God says that God has already given you everything that pertains to life and godliness. (2 Peter 1:3)
The Word of God says that God has already blessed you with Every spiritual blessing in heavenly places in Christ Jesus (Ephesians 1:3) Fear only comes in when you start to wonder, "Can I really do this?"

Here's the truth: God never asked you to do it. God only asked you to be a vessel so that HE could do it through you. It's His gift. His purpose. His plan. His power. So now your fear is really idolatry. Because for you to be scared that you can't do it really means that you're trusting in your strength and not God's.

God said, "Have I not commanded you?" (Verse 9) That's your "Why". That's your confirmation. That's your security. That's your answer when Satan says, "but what if this doesn't work?" Tell him: It's got to work because God said so.

Pray with me:
Father I thank you for your promise over my life. I am already blessed. Increase my faith so that I can do EXACTLY what you created me to do. Without fear. In Jesus's Name, Amen!

DAY TWELVE

Read Luke 10:38-42

Focus

Do you know what a laser is? Focused light. Jesus commanded us to be light for the world. Regular light just shines but Focused Light can cut through anything.

Are you focused? In your life, job, ministry, marriage; are you really focused on the things that matter? Take your job for instance. Are you fully engaged on the task at hand or are you constantly distracted by Facebook, Instagram, emails, text messages, phone calls, YouTube, Twitter, the Vine videos, Netflix, phone games, or just uncontrollably random daydreaming?

Question: How can you be effective if you're not focused?

In our text Jesus was teaching but Martha was so busy working that she couldn't focus on what Jesus was saying. She was so distracted (focused on the wrong things) that she even had the nerve to fuss at Jesus and tell him what to do!

Do you remember when your mom used to call you when you were little but you were so focused on what you were doing that she practically had to shout your name before you responded? That's how Jesus feels. He's screaming your name every day, desperately wanting to spend time with you but we're so busy with everything else that we can't hear him. Take some time today (even if it's only ten minutes) and dedicate it to focusing/Meditating on God. Just listen silently for His voice and watch God EXPLODE in your life!

Pray with me:
Father, I love you. I will give you quality time today. Speak to me Lord. In Jesus's Name, Amen.

DAY THIRTEEN

Read Matthew 7:1-5

Glass Houses

Isn't it funny how it's so easy to see other people's flaws and yet so hard to see our own?

Jesus said, "Why are you looking at the speck in your brother's eye when there is a Log in your eye? Hypocrite!!! First get the beam out of your eye, then you will be able to see clearly to get the beam out of your brother's eye."

The truth is that none of us are perfect. And all of us have a full time job trying to work on our imperfections.

We should be humble and understanding when it comes to other people's flaws. But we're not. We're mean and judgmental and harsh and angry. As if their sin is somehow worse than our sin.

Jesus basically said "people who live in glass houses shouldn't throw stones."

And we all live in glass houses.

So the next time you're about to talk badly about someone, imagine Jesus having a similar conversation about you...

Pray with me:
Father forgive me for judging others and excusing myself. Help me to work on me and love on them. In Jesus's Name, Amen.

DAY FOURTEEN

Read Matthew 7: 13-20

Good or Bad Fruit?

Yesterday we talked about not judging, but let me balance the discussion. "Sinners" love to say stuff like, "You're not supposed to judge" and "Only God can judge me". They use these phrases to ease their conscious about their sinful lifestyle. Jesus said, "Judge not", but after that Jesus turned right back around in the SAME chapter and said "Beware of false prophets. You'll know them by their fruit." Jesus basically said some people are DIRTY and if you watch them long enough they'll prove it! Jesus actually called them "bad trees". But isn't it "judging" to call someone a bad tree? The answer is very simple. When Jesus said "Judge not" he didn't mean "never say anything to anyone about their sin"; He meant "Don't condemn". (Check the Greek). Clearly He commands us to "discern" the fruit that we see in people's lives and govern ourselves accordingly. But the bigger question is, "Why are you so focused on what other people are doing wrong anyway?"

So, to summarize, if I love you then I will definitely call out your sin and pray WITH you as we walk this Christian journey together. I have a Spiritual responsibility to call out sin, I just don't have God's permission to CONDEMN you because of it. So if you're looking to "judge" someone's fruit, the mirror is a good place to start!

Pray with me: Father I thank You that You have forgiven my sin. God, I submit every thought, word and action to You as fruit for Your inspection and judgment. In Jesus's Name, Amen!

DAY FIFTEEN

Read Psalms 37:4

Happy

Are you really happy?

I didn't ask "Do you have joy?" (Even though we know there's a difference) Because sometimes "churchy" people are miserable but they lie to themselves and say "I may not be happy but at least I have joy!" No you don't.
A lot of people live their lives waiting for Friday; waiting for payday; waiting for their birthday; waiting for vacation; waiting for a happy hour... (Oops!)
Because the truth is, what you're really waiting for is the chance to enjoy your life. Now it's true that life won't always be a bed of roses, but the Word of God says, "Delight yourself in The Lord", "Rejoice in The Lord always", "Joy unspeakable and full of glory". Proverbs 3:13 says HAPPY is the man that findeth wisdom and the man that getteth understanding.
Bottom line:
You're not supposed to walk around with this "hidden joy" deep down on the inside that nobody can see unless you tell us.
(By the way, The world knows what happiness is. We're not fooling anybody. :o) Let's fall in love (again) with Jesus today and let Him show us what love and happiness really look like!

Pray with me:
Father I love you. Please shower me with your love today. Let me feel like I'm the apple of your eye. Make me truly happy in You. In Jesus's Name, Amen.

DAY SIXTEEN

Read Acts 2:5-8

God Culture

A few years ago Donald Sterling's racist comments made the issue of race came to the forefront in the NBA. But have you noticed that you NEVER hear about race issues in the NBA? If there was ever a "rainbow coalition" of races and ethnicities it's found in the National Basketball Association. And I believe that the church can find a clue in the unity that exists in the NBA. Whether you're White, Black, Brown, Puerto-Rican or Haitian, HUMAN BEINGS have to discipline themselves to be able to play basketball.

Whether you're black or white, giving up McDonalds everyday so that you can get into playoff shape is hard for everybody. *What's my point? Basketball is a CULTURE that supersedes whatever culture you were born into. Because I don't care what you used to eat "back home"; if it doesn't help you run faster or jump higher, you've got to give it up if you want to stay in the NBA. So here we have a culture of people giving up their differences for the goal of conforming to one image: the image of a champion. Now if basketball players can adapt and transcend to form one culture, shouldn't Christians be able to do the same? Even more so? The bible said that there were dozens of nationalities in Jerusalem on the day of Pentecost and they all heard ONE message; they were all baptized into ONE Name. If the world can come together over *basketball* surely Christians can come together over Christ.

Pray with me: Jesus please BE my culture today. Don't let me identify with Anything more than I identify with you. In Jesus's Name, Amen.

DAY SEVENTEEN

Read John 20:19-22

They Didn't Know

What you don't know _can_ hurt you. I remember when my wife
just started her last job and she was supposed to get her first
paycheck on a Friday. Her job told us that the first check would
be a paper check and that the subsequent ones would be direct
deposit. So, Friday came but... No check!
I was hot! My wife was upset but she said they were mailing the
check from Georgia so we just had to wait. Saturday came... No
check. Monday came... No check. At this point I'll admit, I was
panicking. I mean, we are eating leftovers and budgeting which
trips to take in which car and everything!
Then my wife says, "let me just check my account and see if
they put it in there." "But babe," I said, "I thought they were
gonna send a paper check....?" But when she checked the atm,
the money was there. It had been there the _whole time_. We were
living like paupers when we could have been "balling"!
The disciples in our text were the same way. Jesus had risen
from the dead and they were hiding in a secret room. They were
supposed to be turning the world upside down and they were
cowering in fear. Jesus had to come and _tell_ them that they had
the POWER to change the world. It's time for you to walk in the
fullness of your calling. Don't waste another second living
beneath the promises of God. Love, Joy and Peace is already in
your account! And Because of the blood of Jesus, you can access
them today!

_Pray with me: Father I thank you for everything your
sacrifice bought me. Please don't let me miss anything that
you died to give me. In Jesus's Name, Amen!_

DAY EIGHTEEN

Read Luke 1:39-45

Baby Jump

Mary had a miracle pregnancy. So did Elizabeth. Mary's Son was going to be ridiculously famous. So was Elizabeth's. Mary's Son was gonna die a horrible death. So was Elizabeth's.

What's my point? Mary and Elizabeth had similar destinies. They could relate on a level that few other people could. They could encourage one another, challenge one another and ultimately experience that affirmation that you only feel in the presence of someone that is truly like you.

They were so alike that when Mary came to visit Elizabeth, her baby literally jumped in the womb.

In this life you need to find somebody that makes your "baby jump". Find someone that stirs up your gift every time they come around. Find someone that can make you laugh and cry and think and grow and change... All at the same time.
Love on them, listen to them, encourage them, walk with them. They are your gifts from God.

Who do you have in your life that makes your baby jump?

Pray with me:
Father I thank you for divine hook ups! I thank you for twins in the spirit. Father send me someone who makes my baby jump and help me to stir them up as well. In Jesus's Name, Amen.

DAY NINETEEN

Read Psalms 24:1; Psalms 50:10-12

Lack or Abundance?

The first rule of economics is scarcity. There is not enough of anything to give everybody enough. Some people have to be rich while others are poor. Some people have to throw food away while others starve. Some people have to use up all of the world's natural resources while third world countries bathe in the water they drink from. All because of scarcity.

So, I can't give because if I give there won't be enough for all of us-Scarcity. God doesn't really want ME to be successful. I mean, there are SO many millionaires out there.... I mean... Everybody can't be rich... Scarcity. The greatest lie the devil ever told.
If you never read anything else that I write, Read This:
THERE IS MORE THAN ENOUGH *BLESSING* FOR EVERYONE TO BE ABUNDANTLY BLESSED!!!!!!

We serve an abundant God. We live in an infinite universe. God is eternal: from everlasting to everlasting. Words like: "Lack", "Scarcity", "Shortage", "Recession", "Depression".... These words have NO MEANING in the Kingdom of God.

Pray with me:
Now to Him who is able to do exceedingly abundantly above all that we ask or think, according to the power that works in us, to Him be glory in the church by Christ Jesus to all generations, forever and ever. Amen.

DAY TWENTY

Read Psalms 51; Romans 8:1

The Power of Conviction

Since you've become a Christian you've probably made some mistakes. It happens. Every time you get a new revelation or a desire to do better, the temptation to go back to your old ways will always be there.

Sometimes God really blesses you (like David) and you know that you "know better" but you still mess up. And THAT'S when the enemy comes in with a spirit of condemnation and says "You were never delivered. You don't deserve God's love. You're nothing but a dirty sinner."

But can I tell you a secret? God doesn't send condemnation, He sends conviction.

What does that mean? That means that the very fact that you feel remorse in your spirit is PROOF that you DO belong to God and His spirit is *alive* and *active* in you. The true sinner can sin and feel no remorse. The fact that you can feel God loving you back to a higher standard proves that you belong to Him!

So the next time Satan (literally "the accuser") tries to call you trifling and unworthy, you tell him "Thanks for reminding me! Isn't it Amazing that God loves me anyway!"

Pray with me:
Father I thank you for your redeeming Grace. I thank you for your Holy Spirit that lives in me and tells me when I am wrong. Help me not to Quench your Holy Spirit but to submit to Him. In Jesus's Name, Amen!

DAY TWENTY-ONE

Joshua 1:3-9

Go Get It; NOW!

You have prayed. You have asked. You have waited for your prophetic word; for your confirmation.

Here it is:

Go get it. Now!

The promised land is waiting for you. You don't need permission, revelation or direction.

God has already given you "everything that pertains to life and godliness." (2 Peter 1:3)

God has already "blessed you with every spiritual blessing in heavenly places in Christ Jesus". (Ephesians 1:3)

So stir up the Gift, press toward the mark and Believe that you will prosper and be in good health even as your soul prospers. And do it now. Because God said so. (Joshua 1:9)

Pray with me:
Jesus thank you for your promises. Forgive me for living as if you hadn't already blessed me. Jesus died and rose and He lives. As He lives through me today, nothing will be able to stand in "our" way! In Jesus's Name, Amen!

DAY TWENTY-TWO

Read Acts 12:1-5, 11-16

Do You Believe?

When you pray for God to do things, do you really believe that He is going to do them?
When you pray for the sick do you really EXPECT them to get better? Or if they do get better, are you looking for some medical explanation?

....Do you even pray for the sick?

When you pray for a financial blessing and a family member drops by to give you some money, do you give God glory or just assume the family member would have done it anyway?
We claim to be people of faith but our lives seem ridiculously ordinary...
In the text, several disciples were praying for Peter's miraculous release from prison. But when he WAS released and showed up at the door, they didn't believe it. They actually accused the servant girl of being crazy when she said that Peter was at the door.

Don't miss God's next miracle in your life because you are praying for something that you really don't believe is possible...

Pray with me:
Father, I thank you that you are a God of miracles. With you, all things are possible. Increase my faith Lord, In Jesus's Name, Amen!

DAY TWENTY-THREE

Read Genesis 50:15-20

I'm Starting To Believe

Has anybody ever done you wrong? I mean really did something trifling and nasty and just mean spirited to you? Has anybody ever done anything to you that was so bad that you believe it messed up your life? Yeah, me too.

I think the hero of our text can relate though. And while people may have been mean to us, his brothers ACTUALLY threw him into a pit! And then brought him out only to sell him into slavery!!! But by the time we get to our text, Joseph is very loving and forgiving. How could he do that? Because he believed.

He believed that all things work together for good... He believed that no weapon formed against him would prosper... He believed that The Lord would perfect that which concerned him...

Can I tell you a secret? <u>Bitterness is only for people who DON'T believe that God is in control.</u> If I truly believed that every attack was an elevation in disguise then how could I be mad at my attackers? If you believed that God would bless you every time they hated on you, wouldn't that change your mind toward haters? Well guess what? That's EXACTLY what He said. "Blessed are you when men shall revile you and persecute you and say all manner of evil against you falsely for my sake. Rejoice and be exceedingly glad for great is your reward in heaven." It's time to start believing...

Pray with me:

Father, I thank you for my haters. I thank you for everything you taught me through them. Help me to be better and not bitter in Jesus's Name, Amen.

DAY TWENTY-FOUR

Read Numbers 11:4-10

Are You Making Yourself Unhappy?

Anybody ever thought that your life would be somewhere different "by now"? Me too. When I was turning 35, I had no children, no house, a borrowed car and I had just lost the job that I worked for the last 7 years of my life. This was not exactly the way I planned it! But I DID have a beautiful wife, a healthy body, a brand new ministry that God was really blessing and unlimited potential... But still the picture I had in my mind was different... In my mind, my life played out totally differently. And if I'm not careful I can find myself meditating on my life NOT being the way I drew it up. (I'm sure that none of you do that) But that is a recipe for "stolen happiness."

Let me share with you something that a preacher told me a long time ago, "When God doesn't do what you want him to do THAT'S when you ought to shout! Why? Because that means that God has something so amazing in store for you that He HAD to say no to *your* dream; because your dream was NOTHING compared to His *Vision!*" Let that sink in...

So the next time you find yourself feeling sorry for the way your life is turning out, remember two things: 1. He's not through 2. All things are working together for your good. And 3. (I know, I know)... No good thing will He withhold from those who walk uprightly. Get this in your Spirit: You are EXACTLY where God wants you to be. Stop making yourself unhappy. Meditate on good things. Keep speaking life and watch God work!

Pray with me: Father we thank you for your grace. Your plans for us are amazing. We believe that you're working on our behalf right now. We won't complain like the Israelites. We trust you, in Jesus's Name, Amen.

DAY TWENTY-FIVE

Read 1 Samuel 3:1-10

Speak Lord

Hearing from God is not an exact science.

God doesn't usually speak to us in an audible voice. But even if He did, we could still miss Him just like Samuel did.

Here's the point: Samuel heard God's voice. But he wasn't familiar with God's voice. So he reassigned God's voice to someone that he was familiar with: Eli. A lot of times God will speak to us but we will seek human confirmation before we believe it.

Now Samuel was lucky. Eli told him to go back and listen to God. But how many of us have received HORRIBLE advice from friends when we should have just done what God said in the first place???

God CAN speak through a human but he can also speak directly to you. Learn to hear His voice no matter what method He uses.

Pray with me:
Father, speak to me today. Whatever the method, whatever the message, help me to listen and obey. In Jesus's Name, Amen.

DAY TWENTY-SIX

Read Hebrews 5:11-14

Practice Makes Perfect

It's not easy to hear from God.

When you first get saved, his voice seems clear but as you continue to grow, if you're not intentional about listening to his voice, it will get harder and harder to hear. Then your flesh will also speak to you and try to get you to obey it. Then Satan and his suggestions will also speak and try to get you to obey them.

Here's the truth: Every spirit is not the Holy Spirit. Every voice that you hear is not the Shepherd's voice. Every desire that you feel is not a Godly one.

Hebrews 5:14 says:
"But solid food belongs to those who are of full age (mature), that is, those who by reason of use have their SENSES EXERCISED to discern both good and evil."

You have to practice hearing from God.

More on this tomorrow...

Pray with me:
Father I thank you that you desire to speak with me. Please block out all distractions and teach me how to discern your voice. In Jesus's Name, Amen.

DAY TWENTY-SEVEN

Read Revelation 20:12-15, 2 Corinthians 5:10, Hebrews 9:27

The Judge

I hate going to court. I have to be honest and say that I have spent more time in court than I wanted to because of a heavy foot. (Pray Saints!!!) One of the reasons that I hate court is because the judge can do whatever they want! They can get smart with you, but if you get smart, they hold you in contempt. The officer can say that you were driving recklessly and his word is law.

What am I saying? Am I starting a petition to abolish the court system? No, I'm talking about the power of the court. The bottom line is, when you get in that courtroom, whatever the judge says goes. Whether you agree or not is irrelevant.

What scares me now is that so many people think that their opinion matters when it comes to what God requires. I hear so many people respond to God's warnings by saying "Well, I just don't believe in that!" Who cares what you believe?! You don't have to believe in gravity either. But that doesn't mean jumping off the Empire State Building without a parachute won't kill you. At the end of the day, God has his own rules, his own standards and his own court. He WILL judge. And he will sentence. I love you too much not to tell you the truth.

Pray with me: (if you still want to!)
Father, I am guilty of putting my standards over your standards. I have lied to myself and said that your unconditional love was an excuse to live in sin. Please forgive me and create in me a clean heart that I might please you in my living. In Jesus's Name, Amen.

DAY TWENTY-EIGHT

Read Luke 20:20-26

Taxes

April 15th is a "special" day. It's a day we all look forward to, (Sarcasm font) The deadline to pay taxes! Taxes are necessary to run the government. They pay for schools and roads and teachers and firemen and such... But some people still Hate to pay taxes. Most of us understand that the government has to take a percentage of our wages in order to operate. We may gripe a little but we accept it. But there is another "tax" that supports another "government" that we seem to have problems with: Tithing.

A tithe is giving 10% of ALL of your income to The Lord to support the work of His Kingdom on earth. The Lord commands us to bring HIS tithe to the local storehouse so that His *government* on earth can be financed. It never ceases to amaze me how many "Christians" willingly pay to support a secular government but refuse to pay to support a spiritual one.

Your taxes help pay for earthly soldiers. But you won't help support the spiritual soldiers who war for your soul?

So today, I want you to prayerfully consider starting the spiritual practice of tithing. Scriptural references can be found in Malachi 3:8-10, Matthew 23:23, and 2 Corinthians 9:6-11

Pray with me:
Father, everything I receive came from you and belongs to you. Teach me how to be a good steward of the financial resources that you continuously give me. In Jesus's Name, Amen. (If you have any questions or concerns about tithing, please don't hesitate to email me @
anointedestiny@yahoo.com)

DAY TWENTY-NINE

Read Luke 16:26-35

Noah: Tragedy or Triumph?

The movie "Noah" debuted as the number one movie in the world. But it was just as popular for its controversy as it was for its plot, special effects and acting. The story centers around a man who believes that he hears God say that the world will be destroyed and that he should build an ark to save the animals. But one of the main crises of the film comes up when other people want to get on the ark and Noah says: No. BILLIONS of people die while Noah and his family are safe on the ark. Isn't this wrong? How could God stand by and let Noah do such a horrible thing??? What if I told you God didn't stand by? He ordered it. Then He orchestrated it. The Word even says that God himself shut the door.

At the end of the day brothers and sisters we all have to make a choice. Does *your* perspective control God or does God's perspective control you? What do you do when God does something "Wrong?" Is He now an unjust God because YOU say so? Be careful my friend. That's dangerous territory.

"Well, I wouldn't serve a God who would do that." Fine. Then don't serve Him. But don't presume that you can conform Him into your image of right and wrong. Let us meditate on the story of Noah today and commit to submit to the sovereignty of God. (The real story starts in Genesis 5:28)

Pray with me:

Father, you made us in YOUR image. Please forgive us for trying to remake you in our image. You are sovereign and we are servants. Help us to serve you with a glad heart. In Jesus's Name, Amen.

DAY THIRTY

Read John 11:39-44

Get Ready for Resurrection

Sometimes things die. Relationships die. People die. Dreams die.

But as Christians, we know that physical death is not the end. The popular acronym "Y.O.L.O." (You Only Live Once) was never the case for the Christian. We will be resurrected and live eternally with Jesus.

But as we prepare to face this new day, I want you to think about some things in your life that "died" that you want God to resurrect now. Maybe it was your health; a relationship; your finances. Or maybe it was a dream that God gave you to write a book, record a cd, start a business or reconnect with an estranged family member. Whatever you lost, God said that now is the time to call it forth. This is the season of resurrection. It's time to believe again. The Power of Life and death is in YOUR tongue and whatever you decree SHALL be established. (Proverbs 18:21; Job 22:28)

Grab this WORD by faith: If you can see it, believe it and speak it, you will see the power of God. (verse 40)

Pray with me:
God, you promised to restore the years that the enemy stole. We come in faith agreeing with you that everything he destroyed, you have restored. We will call it restored until we SEE it restored. In Jesus's Name, Amen.

DAY ONE

Read John 11: 1-15, 21
(Verses 1-44 are all good if you feel led to read more)

Did God Fail?

How many times have you prayed for something and it DIDNT happen? How many times did you really depend on God to keep something from happening and it happened anyway?

Did God fail? Did He mess up? Was that a divine "Oopsie"?????

Let me be clear: God never fails. He never makes a mistake. He never gets "caught off guard". The only times it *seems* like He makes a mistake is when we put our desires before His will. His ways are not our ways and his thoughts are not our thoughts. God didn't "miss" your deadline. He didn't forget to come through for you. He simply chose to do something different.

He can do that. He's God.

But if you stick around long enough, you usually find out that you didn't die. The world didn't end. And the thing that you thought you could NEVER overcome... You overcame. By the way, God did that too.

It's not always fun. And it doesn't always make sense to us but all things really do work together for good to them that love The Lord and are the called according to His purpose. God NEVER fails.

Pray with me:
Father, I have judged you when you didn't do what I wanted. I thought you failed. I started to doubt your love and care. I'm sorry. Teach me...
In Jesus' Name, A-men.

DAY TWO

Read Luke 18:9-14

God's Gym

I can't stand planet fitness. I'm sorry. I just can't...
You can't grunt. You can't drop weights. You can't wear a tank
top or carry around a jug of water. In other words, you can't be a
body builder. According to them, people who grunt or lift heavy
weights or look good in a tank top, are intimidating to people
who are new to the gym.
Now while I absolutely hate this policy. I do understand.
Nothing would be worse than some muscle bound idiot scaring
away a person who had a sincere desire to get into shape. It's
same thing with church. Sometimes "church" can be intimidating
because so many people seem to "have it together" spiritually.
And some of them even try to flaunt it! But Jesus said that those
types of people are not sincere. Nobody has it all together. And
anybody who pretends to is a liar; pure and simple.
Jesus accepts you just as you are. And He wants to help you to
grow. If everybody had a six pack already, why would we go to
the gym? If you were already perfect, why would you need God?

Don't let hypocrites keep you from coming to God's gym. We're
all out of shape, but God is the best "trainer" there is.

Pray with me:
Father I thank you that you love me just the way I am. But
Father I also want my lifestyle to please you. Please help
me to rest in your love AND _press towards the mark. In_
Jesus' Name, A-men.

DAY THREE

Read: Matthew 5:43-45, Galatians 6:7-8

Biblical Karma

Whether you call it Karma, sowing and reaping, "The Golden Rule" or simply say "What goes around comes around"; the point is that there is a law at work in this beautiful universe of ours: Whatever you throw out there comes right back to you.

So the next time someone "does you wrong" and you wish that they would get hit by a bus or something, stop and think for a second. If you meditate on "Death by bus" it probably won't hurt them, but it might just hurt you. Negativity breeds negativity.

If you wish something bad on someone, all you're really doing is sending out a signal to draw bad things.... To YOU!

That's why Jesus commanded us to Love people. Forgive people. Bless people. Not because you're a saint but because you have learned the law of Biblical Karma.

Pray with me:
Father, I thank you for my life. I wish nothing but love joy and peace for all of my friends and my enemies. God I pray for those who despitefully use me. I pray great blessing and favor in their lives. God I don't want to see them hurt I want to see myself blessed. Everywhere I look, let my eyes see blessing. In Jesus' Name, A-men.

DAY FOUR

Read Hebrews 4:12-13

How Do I Know?

I used to be fat. I mean really fat. Like "wear a Tshirt to the beach and don't take it off at all fat!"
A few years ago I really started walking in purpose and one of the things that changed was my weight. I couldn't tell just by looking though. One morning I put my clothes on and my belt buckle went to a higher hole than it used to. I remember thinking: Is my waist getting smaller? Then my suits started to look baggy. It got bad!!! I eventually had to buy all new suits. My point is that the only way that I knew for sure that I was losing weight was because I had an "Objective Standard" by which to judge my weight loss.
That's what the Bible is. It's a standard. You may feel like you're a pretty good person but what does that Word say? You may feel like God should be pleased with your life but what does the Bible say about your behavior?
The bottom line is that the Word should be our litmus test to see if we are living the way that God wants us to. You can't just read the scriptures that you like and skip the ones that you don't. That's like going to the gym and skipping the exercises you don't like. (Oops! I felt that in the Spirit! Yes, you need to work everything!!!!) Use the word like a personal trainer. It can get you in shape!

Pray with me:
God please show me your will through your word. And when I find a scripture that I disagree with, help me to submit to your will. I want to grow. In Jesus' Name, A-men.

DAY FIVE

Read Galatians 5:16-25

Who Are You Feeding?

If you put a pitbull up against a Rottweiler in a fight, who would win? Who knows, right?
But let's add the story that the Rottweiler has been training all week while the pitbull has been STARVING ALL week. Now who's gonna win?
Of course the Rottweiler will win now. As a matter of fact, I'm pretty certain that a Chihuahua could defeat a pitbull that hasn't eaten in over seven days!
What's the point? Am I promoting dog fighting? Of course not. But I am making a point about your "Spirit Man".
Every morning you wake up, you have a choice: Am I going to walk in the Spirit (listen to His voice and make Godly choices) or am I going to walk in the Flesh (listen to my own voice and make my own choices).
Every day you MAKE that choice. Several times a day you have to re-make that choice. So when your "flesh" is telling you one thing and your Spirit is telling you another, there is literally a battle going on in your mind for control of your day. And every time you say yes to your flesh you are feeding Satan's control in your life. But every time you say yes to the Spirit, you are feeding God's control in your life. So the question is: Who's gonna win the battle between your spirit and your flesh today? The Answer: The One you feed.
Pray with me:
Father, I know that you have given me the power to choose the good choice; the God choice. Help me today to listen to the Voice that tells me to do the right thing and ignore every other voice. In Jesus' Name, A-men.

DAY SIX

Read 1 Corinthians 2:9, John 14:1-3, Genesis 2:7-8

A Prepared Place

Most people aren't planners. They live life as it comes and they have to deal with a lot of surprises.

Clearly it is true that all of us deal with a certain amount of uncertainty when it comes to our daily lives. Who knows what will happen tomorrow? Will I win a million dollars? Will I get fired? Will I meet the love of my life? Or will I get a speeding ticket? Will I finally discover my purpose in life? Or will I spend one more day aimlessly spinning through life? Honestly who knows?

God does. He knows because He planned it.

1 Corinthians says, "Eyes have not seen... What The Lord has PREPARED for those that love him." John 14 says, "I go to PREPARE a place for you." And Genesis 2 says that God created a garden and there He placed the man He had created. In every instance, nothing was haphazard. No act was random. Every step was a part of the preparation that God made before you got here. You may not be much of a planner but God is. No matter where you are in your life right now, you are EXACTLY where God wants you to be. How do I know? He told me in Jeremiah 29:11

Pray with me:
Father I thank you for my "prepared place". Thank you for my "promised land" of love, peace and joy. Help me to be obedient so that I can walk in everything that you created for me. In Jesus' Name, A-men.

DAY SEVEN

Read 1 Corinthians 13:4-8a
(Preferably in the NIV)

Love Never Fails

We live in a society that throws the word "love" around a lot.
Some of us told boyfriends/girlfriends that we loved them; only
to break up with them when they no longer made us happy.
Some of us told family and friends that we loved them until they
did something "unforgivable". And most of us swear up and
down that we "love" this new pair of shoes or this new outfit or
the latest episode of our favorite show.

But did you really read what the bible says love is? Love is
patient. Love is kind. Love "bears all things". That means that no
matter what, love always forgives. There is nothing that anyone
could do to you that would be unforgivable.
Love doesn't keep a record of wrongs. Ouch!!!! Guilty.
And then it has the nerve to end with "love never fails." (Never
gives up) No matter what, the bible says, real love never stops
believing in someone. It never stops hoping that they will
change. And it never stops loving them even if they don't.

So the next time you "fall" out of love with someone or feel
tempted to justify unforgiveness in your heart towards them, just
ask yourself, "What if the next time I mess up, Jesus didn't
forgive me...?" What if Jesus sent me a text that said "we need to
talk. I'm just not feeling this anymore...."

Pray with me:
Father, teach me how to love. In Jesus' Name, Amen.

DAY EIGHT

Read Matthew 5: 13-16, Acts 1:8

Don't Do. Be.

Jesus said you are the light of the world. You are the salt of the earth.

Light doesn't have to "try" to shine. It just does. Salt doesn't have to struggle to make a difference in your food. All you have to do is shake a little on there and it will naturally make affect its environment.

Jesus called us light and salt. A lot of us are trying too hard. Jesus said "be witnesses." Not "do witnessing".
You're so busy trying to "act right", that everybody can see it's just an act.

When I was in high school, there was a big debate about "acting black" or "acting white". If you were a black kid but you listened to Heavy Metal, you were "acting white". But y response to them was always, "I'm not "acting white" or "acting black". I AM black! Anyway that I act is acting black!"
You ARE a Christian. Jesus really does love you. Stop trying to "act" like one and BE one...

Pray with me:
Father, please teach me how to rest in your love and not try to prove anything to anyone. I know you love me. And I love you too.
In Jesus' Name, A-men.

DAY NINE

Read Ecclesiastes 3:1-11

God's Timing

Timing is everything.

Just ask a baseball player. What's the difference between a strike and a home run? Timing. Let me tell you a secret: a lot of us are frustrated right now because we are looking for the right thing at the wrong time. But the right thing at the wrong time is the wrong thing.
What's the difference between winter and spring? Timing. What's the difference between infancy and maturity? Timing. Some of us are frustrated in our lives because we're looking for springtime blessings in our season of winter. Some of us are frustrated because we want our pre-school teacher to hand out driving permits. (Thank God for timing!)
Let me encourage you: You're not doing anything wrong. God is not mad at you. The reason you don't see flowers blooming is NOT because you're a dirty sinner! It's because it's the wrong season! The reason why preschoolers aren't driving escalades is not because God is punishing them! It's because they're not ready. It's not their season. And I'll throw this in for free: A blessing that you're not prepared to handle is a CURSE.
Verse 11 says that God makes everything beautiful in its own time. Join me in believing that.
Pray with me:
Father, I submit to your timing. Your word says, "No 'good thing' will you withhold from those who walk uprightly." So if you haven't given it to me, I trust that right now it's not a 'good thing'. In Jesus' Name, Amen.

DAY TEN

Read Luke 22:31-34

Bring Out The Best!

Human beings are peculiar.

One of our peculiarities is that we don't always do our best unless we're faced with a challenge. We usually only do enough to get by. I call it "playing to the level of our competition". In other words, if we're playing Michael Jordan, then we bring our "A" game. But if we're playing a little kid, we usually wind up playing way below our potential. Right?

Newsflash: That's why God is allowing Satan to hit you so hard. He's trying to bring out the best in you. If you only deal with light trials then it won't produce a Heavy anointing.

Peter was destined to be a powerful leader in the new church. But in our text he is an arrogant, "wishy-washy" excuse for a disciple. So, how did Jesus transform him into the Pentecost preacher? One Word: PAIN.

So be encouraged! If it feels like you're fighting a Mike Tyson Devil, it's just because God is creating a Muhammad Ali anointing! Rumble, young man Rumble!!!

Pray with me:
Father, forgive me for doing just enough to get by. I know you see greatness in me. Help me to realize it. And I even thank you for the great battles that you sent into my life. Because their very presence means that you believe I'm strong enough to handle them.
In Jesus' name, Amen.

DAY ELEVEN

Read I Kings 17: 1-9

Don't Miss The Shift

There's nothing worse than a missed opportunity.

Most of us wind up missing the 'next' move of God because we fall in love with His last move...
Don't get stuck when the brook dries up, Elijah.
God knew the brook would dry up. But He didn't tell Elijah.
He had already prepared Elijah's next miracle. And this one was going to make a Gentile convert. But it was also going to test Elijah's faith. Question: Are you going to cry and complain because the brook dried up or are you going to listen for God's next word? Are you going to bury your head in despair and doubt or are you going to sharpen your vision so you can SEE God's next move?

Receive this Word: The brook was never meant to last forever. Just like God provided for you there, He will provide for you elsewhere. Don't miss the Shift that God wants to do in your life because you got stuck looking for water in a dry brook. A wise man once said, "When the horse is dead, dismount!" And remember, God didn't fail; the season just ended. Trust God and enjoy your transition to the next chapter of His goodness.

Pray with me:
Father I trust you. Help me not to trust in the blessing but in the "Blesser". Guard my heart and mind in Christ Jesus and help me to always look and listen for the shift. In Jesus' Name, Amen.

DAY TWELVE

Read 2 Kings 6:8-17

Put Your Glasses Back On

I am nearsighted.

I haven't been able to do anything without wearing my glasses since I was in the 5th grade. I only take them off to go to sleep and I keep them beside my bed so I can put them on immediately when I wake up.

One day I got up got ready and actually walked out of the door without my glasses on. I was shocked! I couldn't understand how it happened. I always realize that I don't have them on because I have trouble seeing. But then it dawned on me. I was staying in an extended stay hotel. It's really just one big room. Everything is close together. So I didn't need great vision to operate in this small space. It wasn't until I got outside that I noticed that I didn't have my glasses on. It wasn't until I enlarged my territory that I noticed that my vision was poor.

Some of us have been living inside a small box for so long that we don't even realize that it has affected out vision. Step out on faith. Dream again. Believe again. And watch God enlarge your vision. Put your glasses back on.

Pray with me:
Lord open my eyes. Help me to see in the spirit everything that you are trying to show me. In Jesus' Name, Amen.

DAY THIRTEEN

Read 2 Kings 4:1-7

What's In Your House?

In our text, the man of God told the woman to go get some vessels. He didn't tell her how many to get but he did indicate that she shouldn't just get a few. We don't know how many empty containers she got but we do know that God filled every container she gave Him. When she ran out of empty containers, the oil stopped flowing.

Your prophetic word for the day: God will fill every container you give Him. Proverbs 1:3 says "everything he DOETH shall prosper". (emphasis mine) The reason why most of us aren't seeing the abundance that God promised is because God can't bless what you don't do. God is a God of multiplication. But zero times zero is zero. A million times zero is zero. It doesn't matter how much power God has to multiply your blessings if you never give him anything to bless.

The widow had oil. The widow got jars. The Lord added the increase. What do you have in your house? What spiritual and natural resources have you overlooked while you were "waiting on God"? What billion dollar ideas have you put on the back burner while you desperately pray for God to drop dollar bills from heaven? Use what you have and God will bless what you use. Get busy stirring up the gift that God already gave you and I promise you, God will get busy making your gift make room.

Pray with me:

Father, please forgive me for making excuses. Your word says that you have already given me everything that I need for life and godliness. Help me to realize, access and utilize every gift that you gave me. In Jesus' Name, Amen!

DAY FOURTEEN

Read Ezekiel 37:1-10

Speak Life

Proverbs 18:21 says that death and life are in the power of the tongue. What are you speaking?
God asked Ezekiel one simple question, CAN these bones live? He didn't ask him, "What is their current status?" God knew that the bones were dead. But God isn't bound by our present reality. He can speak things that be not as though they were.
But just like God has the power to speak things into existence, so do we. Do you ever say things like, "Uh-oh, it's gonna be one of those days." How about, "Nothing good ever happens to me. It seems like something is always going wrong. Man, I can't win for losing!" If you have ever said anything like that (and we all have) then you are actually helping Satan to sabotage your destiny.

The bible says Death and life are in your tongue. So today, try to make a special effort to ONLY speak life and see what a difference it makes!

Pray with me:
Lord Jesus, set a guard over my mouth today. Please don't let me speak words of bitterness, frustration or faithlessness. Fill my mouth with good things. Teach me to speak life. In Jesus' Name, Amen.

DAY FIFTEEN

Read John 10:10, Acts 3:19, Nehemiah 8:10b

Take Your Life Back!

Have you ever felt overwhelmed by the monotony of life? Same old, same old over and over again? Have you ever felt like your weeks were too long and your weekends were too short? Have you ever felt like asking. "What's the point?"

Me too.

But even worse, have you ever been in church and felt like it was just as meaningless? Like you were just going through the motions? What if I told you that was not God's will?

What if I told you that God didn't want you to be bored in church? Or at your job, or in your life? What if I told you that God was passionate about pouring joy back into your heart? Can you imagine a life filled with constant excitement, passion and adventure along with peace, love and fulfillment? What if I told you that was already God's plan for your life?
Love. Joy. Peace. Power. Fulfillment. Meaningful Contribution. Divine Favor. Abundant life. This is your birthright in Christ. Start Living...

Pray with me:
Father, please teach me today what you meant when you promised me abundant life. And God, don't just tell me, SHOW me today. In Jesus' Name, Amen.

DAY SIXTEEN

Read Psalms 118:24, Philippians 4:8

T.G.I.M.! (Thank God It's Monday!)

Most people hate Mondays.
But Mondays really aren't the problem. Let me prove it to you. If
I told you that I would give you one million dollars every
Monday for the next year, would you still hate Mondays?
Exactly.
So now that we've established that we don't really hate Mondays,
why is it that we dread them so much? It's because of what they
represent. They represent starting another week. Another week at
a job I may not like. Facing a financial situation I don't like.
Working with people I don't like. Being forced to spend 40 hours
a week in a building I don't like, doing activities I'd rather not be
doing. Sound familiar?
But David had a different attitude. He said "this is the day that
The Lord has made, I will rejoice and be glad in it!"
Does that mean that David didn't have problems?
Of course he did. He was the King of ALL Israel. Clearly he had
More problems than *any* of us have today. So why was he
rejoicing? Because he figured out something that God wants u to
receive today: Whatever you meditate on, you manifest.
So if you start the week thinking, "Ugh! Another Monday..."
Chances are, you will have a day that lines up with what you
projected. But if you start the day with, "Praise God it's Monday!
God is going to do miracles in my life today!" Chances are you'll
have a better day, a better week and a better life.
Pray with me:
Father thank You for this Amazing Day. Give me a reason
to be amazed and awestruck by your power and presence
in my life today. In Jesus' Name, Amen.

DAY SEVENTEEN

Read Psalms 37:4

Happy

Are you really happy? I didn't ask "Do you have joy?" Because sometimes "churchy" people are miserable but they lie to themselves and say "I may not be happy but at least I have joy!"

No you don't.

A lot of people live their lives waiting for Friday; waiting for payday; waiting for their birthday; waiting for vacation; waiting for "happy" hour... But the truth is, what you're really waiting for is the chance to enjoy your life.
Now it's true that life won't always be a bed of roses, but the Word of God says, "Delight yourself in The Lord", "Rejoice in The Lord always", "Joy unspeakable and full of glory". Proverbs 3:13 says HAPPY is the man that findeth wisdom and the man that getteth understanding.

Bottom line: Joy is evident. You're not supposed to walk around with this "hidden joy" deep down on the inside that nobody can see unless you tell us. People know what happiness looks like. We're not fooling anybody. Let's fall in love (again) with Jesus today and let Him show us what happiness really looks like!

Pray with me:
Father I love you. Please shower me with your love today. Let me feel like I'm the apple of your eye. Make me truly happy in You. In Jesus's Name, Amen.

DAY EIGHTEEN

Read Matthew 3:13-17; 4: 1-3

The Power of Identity

Who are you? How do you define yourself? Are you Black or White? Methodist or Baptist? Democrat or Republican? Pro-Life or Pro-Choice? (by the way, it may shock you to hear which one God is...) Do you have a lot of accomplishments? Do you have a degree? Lots of beautiful children? Nice cars? A respectable reputation in the community?

What defines you? How about the identity of your Father...?

The thing that I love about the Father is that He could have said ANYTHING at Jesus' baptism. In fact, He didn't have to speak at all. But out of all the things He could have said; out of all the topics He could have addressed, He chose to say, "You're my Son. And I'm proud of you." Many of us never got a chance to hear our natural Father's say that. But it's powerful. And it had nothing to do with what Jesus did. Because he hadn't done anything yet. God said, "I'm Proud of you", before Jesus worked one miracle or taught one message. The Father's love isn't based on performance, it's based on identity. I love you simply because you're my child. That's who YOU ARE. You're not a democrat. You're not a Baptist. And you're not an opinion about abortion or homosexuality. You are a beloved child of the King.

Pray with me:
Father. Daddy... I lift up my arms and ask to sit in your lap and feel your love and protection. Remind me that you love me today and help me to bask in the glow of your love and Fatherly goodness. In Jesus' Name, Amen.

DAY NINETEEN

Psalms 34:1-3

From Praise to Strength

Have you ever felt weak or insufficient in any area of your life?

Of course you have. We all have. But I'll bet you didn't know that the Bible has the perfect prescription for you to go from weakness to strength in *every* area of your life.

Wanna know what it is? Praise.

Let me break it down… Psalms 22:3 says that God *inhabits* the praises of His people. Psalms 16:11 says "In His *presence* is the fullness of Joy. And Nehemiah 8:10 says the joy of the Lord is your *strength*.

So when you praise you get His presence; in His presence is the fullness of joy and His joy is our strength.

Are you feeling weak or insufficient in any area of your life? Start praising God. And watch His power being to flow in your life.

Pray with me:

Father I bless Your Name. You are worthy. You are amazing. You are magnificent. You are beautiful. You are wonderful. You are my best friend and I love and praise You today. In Jesus' Name, Amen

DAY TWENTY

Acts 10:9-15

Yes Lord.

Have you ever told God no? Have you ever felt led to do something but didn't. Have you ever read a scripture that told you to stop doing something but you ignored it? How do you think God feels about that?

In the Biblical story, a voice told Peter to "Arise, kill and eat". Then Peter responded with three of the strangest words ever recorded in scripture, "not so, Lord".

Sound familiar? We've all said it. But here's the problem… Either you can say, "Not so" or you can say "Lord", but you can't say both. If Jesus is *truly* your Lord then you don't have the authority to tell Him "no". Jesus said "Why do you call me 'lord, lord' but do not do what I say?" (Luke 6:46). I Corinthians 6:19-20 says, "You are not your own. You were bought with a price…" Finally, Jesus said if any man would come after me, let him deny himself, take up his cross and follow me.

The Bottom line is that as long as you're making the decisions in your life then Jesus is not Lord. If you can veto God's word in your heart then He is not God, you are.

God is either "Lord of all" or He's not Lord at all.

Pray with me:

Father I repent for the times I resisted Your Spirit. I repent for telling You "no". Please grant me an obedient heart, a willing spirit and a crucified flesh. In Jesus' Name, Amen!

DAY TWENTY-ONE

2 Peter 1:1-3

You Are Already Blessed

Get this in your spirit: You're not waiting on God. God is waiting on you. Most of us are waiting on God right now to send us something or to bless us with something that we don't have. The problem with that is that it totally contradicts the Word of God. 2 Peter 1:3 says that God has already given us everything that pertains to life and godliness. Translation: We already have everything that we need. Ephesians 4:7 says that every one of us has a gift. That's why the bible says "Stir up the gift that is in you" and "Your gift will make room for you". The gift of God is already inside of you but you have to stir it up. Psalm 1:3 talks about a righteous man and says "Whatsoever he doeth shall prosper" but can I tell you a secret? God can't bless what you don't do. So start acting Blessed! God has given you access to all of His power. (All things are possible to them that believe) you've just got to renew your mind and believe it. Do you remember Peter walking on water? As soon as Jesus gave him permission to come, he already had the power to walk on water. But when he saw the wind and the waves, he forgot that he was already blessed. And here's the crazy reasoning: God can help me walk on water but God can't save me from drowning. Really Peter?! Really?

Renew your mind. Don't let the enemy scare you. You're already blessed.

Pray with me: Father, show me who I am in you. Reveal my new nature and the Blessing of my birthright in you. Reveal your glory in me. In Jesus' Name, Amen.

DAY TWENTY-TWO

Read Matthew 13:53-58, Hebrews 4:2

The Missing Ingredient (Part 1)

The Bible is filled with amazing promises. "Ask and you shall receive; speak those things that be not as though they were; and these signs shall follow them that believe…they will drive out demons, they will speak with new tongues, they will lay hands on the sick and they will recover; greater works than these shall ye do because I go to my father." (Matthew 7:7, Romans 4:17, Mark 16:17, John 14:12)

But if we look at the church today and more specifically our own lives, are we really walking in the power the Bible Promised? Probably not. What's the problem then? Is the Word of God not true? Of course it's true. God is not a man that He should lie and the promises of God are still yea and Amen. So again I ask, what's the problem? Why are we not walking in power? In a word: Unbelief.

Here's what the Bible says: The word of God is living, powerful, sharper than any 2 edged sword. But the Word also says that even though the word is powerful, it won't do you any good unless you mix it with faith. (Hebrews 4:12, Hebrews 4:2)

More on this tomorrow…

Pray with me: Father in the Name of Jesus, Increase my faith and give me an obedient heart to walk in the level of faith that you've already given me. In Jesus' Name Amen.

DAY TWENTY-THREE

Read Matthew 13:53-58, Hebrews 4:2

The Missing Ingredient (Part 2)

Did you read the story in Matthew 13? Isn't that the craziest thing you've ever read?! Let me make this live for you. Jesus has all power. He is willing and able to heal all of their diseases but because of their unbelief, Jesus CANNOT perform the miracles. I want you to be clear as you read this; it does not say that He _chose_ not to. It literally says that the power of God CANNOT FLOW in an atmosphere of unbelief. Prove it to me in the scriptures. Ok.

Matthew 17:19-20 Then his disciples came to him in private and asked, "Why could we not drive it out?" He replied, "Because of your unbelief." Unbelief does not affect God's power. Unbelief just affects our access to it. Get this in your spirit: Faith activates the power of God. That's why the Bible says All things are possible to them that believe. Be it unto you according to our faith. Your faith has made you whole. The power of God is literally sitting and waiting on a child of God to access it by faith. He has already given you the power. You just have to walk in it. He has already given you the gift, you just have to stir it up! Do you remember the woman with the issue of blood? She accessed the healing power of God without even asking Jesus! 1) She believed, 2) she spoke in her heart that her healing would happen when she touched Jesus' hem and 3) She touched him and was healed. Believe it, speak it, act on it. That's the antidote for unbelief. That's faith. That's the missing ingredient.

Pray with me: Father I thank you for the miraculous power of faith. Give me a heart to believe and receive your promises for my life. In Jesus' Name, Amen.

DAY TWENTY-FOUR

Read Deuteronomy 30:11-20

User Error

Sometimes technology frustrates me. It always seems to be breaking down and not doing the things that it's supposed to do. But the worst part is that when I call the IT guy, he tells me that it's "User Error". In other words, my computer is working fine, I just don't know what I'm doing! But "user error" doesn't just stop with technology. If I had a nickel for every time I heard somebody say, "I just don't know what God wants me to do", I'd have a lot of nickels! A lot of times we say "I don't have the answers." But if we do an "obedience check", the truth is that we *do* have the answers, we just don't like what Jesus said. We're only willing to follow Jesus at the points where His will intersects ours.

God wants to bless me? Great! God loves me? Awesome! Deny yourself and take up your cross? Um, get back to me… Love your enemies and pray for those who despitefully use you? Um, No. Just no.

Moses knew that this problem would arise. That's why he said, "What I am commanding you today is not too difficult or beyond your reach." Beloved, before you question the promises of God or worse the integrity and goodness of God, make sure you're following the instructions. If your Christian Life isn't working, I can guarantee you that it's "User Error".

Pray with me: Father, please give me a heart of obedience. Help me to do your will with my whole heart. Thank you that your commandments are not grievous. They are life. In Jesus' Name, Amen.

DAY TWENTY-FIVE

Read John 4:4-14

I'm Thirsty

Do you remember being a little kid playing outside? Running and sweating and playing until you got tired? If it was a hot day, it would only be a matter of time before you called "time out" so that you could get something to drink! If you were like me as a kid, you would start off trying to drink soda or Kool-Aid, but after you drank a whole cup of some sugary liquid, you discovered something strange… you were still thirsty. No matter how much Kool-Aid you drank, it would never really quench your thirst. Because even though it tasted good, it didn't have the power to replenish your body after you poured out all of your energy. In order to have the energy to go back out and continue playing you need to drink some water. I know what you're thinking: I already knew that. True. But did you also know that your soul gets thirsty? It does. In fact, just by living life every day, you pour out lots of spiritual and emotional energy. And you can feel it when you're drained. Most people try to quench their spiritual thirst with drugs, alcohol, sex, pleasing others or some other hobby. But just like that Kool-Aid, they find that these things don't really satisfy their true thirst. Only Jesus, the Living Water can satisfy the thirsting of your soul.

Are you thirsty?

Pray with me: Father I thank you for providing me with living water. Your word says that you lead me beside still waters and you will restore my soul. Let me drink from the well of your Spirit today. In Jesus's Name, Amen.

DAY TWENTY-SIX

Read John 10:10, John 18:37

The Power of Purpose

One of my mentors always said "If you don't know the purpose of a thing, you are subject to misuse it".

Imagine with me that you have never heard of a microphone. When you see one for the first time, how would you know what it was? Suppose that you held it in your hand and thought it was a hammer. You thought it was a hammer because you know about hammers and that's the closest thing you can associate with what you have in your hand. Imagine further that you started banging nails with the microphone. That would be crazy right? But the worst part is that a microphone would actually make a pretty decent hammer. But every time you used it as a hammer, you would be destroying the purpose for which it was created.

Some of us are like that microphone. We don't know our purpose so we're stuck in a dead end job, wasting our lives 8 hours at a time. And every time you go to a job that you hate, a little piece of your destiny is being destroyed. Isn't it worth it to start fasting and praying to find out what your purpose is? That's what made Jesus so powerful. He knew exactly what His purpose was. And He never deviated from it.

Got purpose?

Pray with me: Father I thank you for creating me with purpose. Please help me to figure out what you have called me to do and then help me to get busy doing it. In Jesus's Name, Amen.

DAY TWENTY-SEVEN

Read Jeremiah 1:4-10

The Power of Purpose (Pt 2)

Purpose is a powerful thing.

Purpose brings direction, motivation and focus. When you don't know what you're called to do, your life doesn't have much meaning or direction. There is no "right" highway to take if the destination doesn't matter. But the moment I declare that I am headed to D.C. then the pathway becomes clear. Purpose also creates motivation. Human beings are teleological creatures. That just means that we like to begin with the end in mind. And we have trouble getting motivated when we don't know what we're going to get out of it. Knowing your purpose means that Monday morning at 9:00 is no longer a time that you hate. It becomes transformed into a moment that you can't wait for. Too good to believe? Nope. That's just the power of purpose.

Lastly, purpose provides focus. Focus is the ability to block out distractions. One of my favorite quotes is, "A car will never reach its destination if it stops to throw rocks at every dog that barks." In other words, if you're going to be successful at reaching your goals, you have to be able to block out every force that would seek to distract you from getting there. When you are sure of your purpose, you can always get refocused by remembering what really matters.

Got Purpose?

Pray with me: Father I thank you for my purpose. Please reveal your perfect will for my life. Give me direction, motivation and focus. Help me to advance your Kingdom and please your heart. In Jesus's Name, Amen.

DAY TWENTY-EIGHT

Read Psalms 1:1-3, 2 Corinthians 6:14-18

The Elevator

Have you ever gotten into an elevator while you were on your cell phone? Did the reception get bad? Did the call drop? As frustrating as that is, there is something about getting on an elevator that just doesn't allow you to stay connected to the person that you were previously talking to. Life is the same way. When God chooses to elevate you to the next level, sometimes He breaks your connection to the people that were on the last level. Especially if they are negative, carnal or unwilling to grow with you. It doesn't mean that they are bad people, it just means that you r connection wasn't meant to survive your elevation. Sometimes elevation requires separation.

Another thing about an elevator is that it has limited space and a weight limit. Translation: You can't take everybody with you. If you have too many people in the elevator, one of two things will happen: 1) the door won't close and you won't be able to start moving up; or 2) you exceed the weight capacity and the elevator crashes, hurting everyone inside.

Don't fight the process. Accept the truth: Everyone can't come with you.

Pray with me:

Father I thank you for my elevation. Lord, if I am doing anything to stand in Your way, please show me. I want to be in Your will and I'm excited about the next level! Father, I'm ready. In Jesus's Name, Amen.

DAY TWENTY-NINE

Read 1Peter 2:9-10, Matthew 5:13-16

X-Men

You're different. You're not like the others. You try to blend in but you always stand out. You are a peculiar person because there is something inside you that cannot be hidden. There is a power inside you that is yearning to be exposed. You're not just human. You are more. No, you're not a mutant; you're a Christian. And because you are a Christian that means that the power of the Holy Spirit lives on the inside of you. You are salt. You are light. You couldn't hide it even if you wanted to. You were born to stand out.

You're also different because you're not who you used to be. The bible says, "If any man be in Christ, he is a new creature. Old things are passed away, behold all things are become new." Every Christian is an "X-Man" in the truest sense. We are all X-liars, X-fornicators, X-gossipers, X-fighters, X-haters. If you're a Christian then you're not who you used to be. You are a new creature; born again…with Power.

Thank God for X-Men.

Pray with me:

Father I thank you that my past is over and I'm not who I used to be. Help me to walk in the newness of life that you have given me. I'm not the old man any more. I am a new creature in You. Teach me what that means and help me to walk in it. In Jesus's Name, Amen.

DAY THIRTY

Read Philippians 2:13, Ephesians 3:20 and Galatians 2:20

The POWER of YOU

Most of us are familiar with Ephesians 3:20. We love to quote the verse that says God can do "exceeding, abundantly ABOVE what we ask or think…' But have you ever noticed that the verse doesn't end there? The verse goes on to say, "According to the power that works in you." Could it be that we're not seeing the Power of God manifesting in our lives because we are waiting on God while God is waiting on us?

If God put the power in us than He expects US to use it. Too often we are waiting on a "move of God". But can I tell you a secret? God lives inside you. You ARE a move of God. God told YOU to have dominion. God gave YOU authority to tread on serpents and scorpions and all the power of the enemy. God told YOU to speak those things that be not as though they were. God said that Death and Life are in the power of YOUR tongue.

Stop asking God to move your mountain when God told you to move it yourself. (Mark 11:23) Stop asking God to fight the darkness in your life when He told YOU to be light. (Matthew 5:14) God gave you power. Are you using it?

Pray with me:

Father, forgive me for asking you to do things that you have empowered me to do. Give me the faith and boldness to walk in the power of your Word. In Jesus's Name, Amen!

DAY ONE

Read Acts 1:8; 2 Timothy 3:1-5

Plug-In

Have you ever bought a device that needed electricity to work?

Whether it's a blender or a tv; a refrigerator or a laptop, there are a lot of things that you can buy that won't work unless you have power. It doesn't matter that you bought it. It doesn't matter that it's assembled correctly. It doesn't matter that you really want to use it. If you don't have power the device won't work.
Your Christian walk is the same way.
Jesus told his disciples NOT to teach, preach or even leave Jerusalem until they received power from on high. They had the message. They had the methodology. They had even seen it modeled as they had obediently followed Jesus. All the pieces were in place but without the power of the Holy Spirit, the gospel would have never spread.

What's the point?

A lot of you are facing problems right now. And the answer to your problems is not the doctor. Not counseling. Not psychotropic drugs. Not more money. Not a better job. Not a new house or car. The answer is the POWER of the Holy Spirit. Period.

Pray with me:
Father I thank you for the AMAZING power of your Holy Spirit. Please teach me how to access it. In Jesus's Name, Amen!

DAY TWO

Read Philippians 3:10

Hedonism" (The Pursuit of Pleasure)

I truly believe that one of the biggest sins of the church is when we tell people that the purpose of relationship with God is to escape pain.

All you have to do is turn to TBN or The WORD Network and you'll hear sermons like:
"Seven ways to be blessed"
"God wants you to enjoy your life"
"No more pain: The Struggle is Over!"

Please allow me to burst that bubble. While it is true that God does want you to be blessed; God does NOT want to take away all your pain. Sometimes God *uses* pain to speak to you.

If you believe that the purpose of the gospel is for God to bless you and take away all your troubles then you're probably having a horrible time understanding your life as a Christian. But if you, like Paul, understand that suffering is one of the ways that God: 1) speaks to you and 2) Makes you more like Christ, then you might be on your way to knowing God more intimately.

Pray with me:
Father, pain does NOT feel good. But if painful circumstances will somehow help me get to know you better then I will submit to your plan.
In Jesus's Name, Amen!

DAY THREE

Read Genesis 25:29-34, Hebrews 12:14-17

Temporary

Have you ever heard the saying, "Never make a permanent decision based on temporary feelings"?

Esau obviously hadn't.
In our text, Esau sells his invaluable birthright for a bowl of stew. That's right. One meal.... Of stew. And the bible says that after he sold it, he tried to get it back. He sought repentance with tears but could not get it. But before we look down on Esau, how many times have we made permanent decisions based on very temporary feelings?
How many divorces have happened because people got upset in a moment and did something they would later regret? How many marriages happened based on temporary infatuation? How many children were conceived..? How many jobs were quit...? How many crimes were committed because people made permanent decisions with lasting consequences based on temporary feelings?

So as you start your day today, be mindful of your feelings but don't be led by them. Never make a permanent decision based on temporary feelings...And ALL feelings are temporary.

Pray with me:
Father I thank you for your Holy Spirit who is greater than my feelings. Father, lead me through your Holy Spirit and never through the feelings in my flesh. In Jesus's Name, Amen.

DAY FOUR

Read Deuteronomy 30:15-19

Simple, but not easy

How do I lose weight? Eat less. Exercise more.

How do I have a lasting marriage? Don't get divorced.

How can I be happy? Focus on things that make you happy and stop focusing on the things that don't.

The greatest truths in life all have one thing in common: They are simple, but not easy. Just because you know HOW to do something doesn't mean that you actually have the motivation to actually do it.
God told the children of Israel that all they had to do was choose life but they spent the rest of their lives "choosing" death.

Every day of our lives God gives us the same choices. The rules are simple. Follow God's commands and prosper. Disobey Him and suffer.

But we usually suffer...

Only the Holy Spirit can help us live a life that is pleasing to God and successful for us. Because mastering the "God Life" is simple but it's not easy.

Pray with me:
Father I thank you that your commands are simple. But God I pray for the supernatural strength to perform them. In Jesus's Name, Amen.

DAY FIVE

Read Genesis 12:1-7

Will you go?

God told Abram to leave everything that he knew and start walking... Somewhere...
God's actual words were "to a land that I will show you". "Will show you"... As in future tense.
As in, I'm asking you to leave everything you know, everything that's comfortable and go to a land that I'm not even gonna tell you. Just start walking and turn left when I say left.

Wow.

How many of us could have THAT level of obedience? Could you just quit your job, leave your extended family, pack up the spouse and/or kids and just start driving 40 West...? What about money? What about a place to live? Where the heck are we even going?
Abraham may or may not have asked these questions. We don't know. All we know is that he went. God spoke and he went. God is still calling people today to radical obedience.

Will you go?

Pray with me:
Father, I have said so many times, "I'll go where you want me to go, I'll do what you want me to do." But today father, I am ready to put action to my faith. Whether you want me to leave the state or just leave my state of mind; lead me, I'll go. In Jesus's Name, Amen.

DAY SIX

Read Hebrews 5:12-14

The Milky Way

When a child is first born they can't eat hamburgers and French fries. Their bodies can't handle it yet. Infants use milk to provide their nutritional needs. Milk is great for babies but how would YOU like to go on a milk diet for the next couple of weeks? Crazy right?! Because milk can only sustain a baby. It's a horrible diet for adults.

That's what a lot of us are doing in the Spirit. We're stuck on milk. "Milky" sermons are sermons that only talk about God's love and blessings and joy. Sermons that make you feel all warm and fuzzy but leave you with no sense of calling and destiny and responsibility to fight for the Kingdom of God.

Now don't get me wrong, all of that stuff is good and foundational- just like milk. And the bible even commands us to desire the sincere milk of the word. But you can't spend your WHOLE life reading John 3:16 ONLY! People are dying. Satan is waging war against marriage, war against families, war against unborn children, war against the church, war against the poor, war against the Kingdom of God! Somebody has to graduate from nursery school and join the army of God. Will it be you? Let us go on to maturity....

Pray with me:

Father I know you love me. I know that you want to bless me and that your deepest desire is intimacy with all of your children. Father help me to fulfill my calling to add to my faith virtue and to virtue knowledge. Help me to not just be a "child of the King", but a "Warrior for the Kingdom."
In Jesus's Name, Amen.

DAY SEVEN

Read Joshua 1:8, Galatians 6:9

God is not punishing you

God doesn't punish people. (The only "punishment" that God will ever do is send people to hell.) Every "punishment" that happens to you on this earth is a result of your actions.

If you jump up in the air, God didn't pull you back down, gravity did. If you eat sweets all day every day, God didn't give you diabetes, you did.

Why is this important? Because if you think God is mad at you, you won't pray for his help when the devil attacks you. Satan will lie to you and say you're under attack because you sinned and God is angry with you. And you HAVE sinned. But God doesn't punish you with *demonic* strongholds. But satan wants you to think that He does.

So the next time you're wondering whether this sickness is God's will or whether this financial struggle is God's way of "teaching you something", do me a favor: Start repenting of your sin and rebuking the enemy in your life and see what happens. Because my Bible says, "If my people who are called by my name will humble themselves and pray as seek my face and turn from their wicked ways, then I will hear from heaven and forgive their sins and heal their land. Let's stop making excuses for the enemy and let's start praying and believing that God will heal the land.

Pray with me:

Father in the name of Jesus, I bind every sickness, disease, stronghold, attack, demonic assignment and evil word that has EVER been spoken over my life; even if it came from me. Father I declare that I will be the head and not the tail and that my whole household will be blessed as we obey your will. In Jesus's Name I pray and give thanks, Amen!

DAY EIGHT

Read 1 John 2: 15-17

Success 101

What is success? Is it driving a certain car? Living in a certain house or neighborhood? Perhaps it's having enough money to enjoy the "finer things" in life or retire well. Let me ask it this way, what are some things that you HAVE to have in order to consider yourself successful? Could you be a success if you didn't have a car? What if you were getting souls saved by the hundreds but you were homeless? What if you could lay hands on the sick and they would recover but the repo man was coming to "lay hands" on your car because you couldn't make the payment? Still feeling successful?

While it sounds cute to say that money or houses or nice things are NOT a part of our definitions of success, the truth is that for most of us they are. So it makes John's words particularly poignant when he says the things that you want (lust of the flesh), the pretty things you want to buy (lust of the eyes) and the status that you want to achieve in life (the pride of life) are ALL from the devil. Jesus said seek ye first the Kingdom of God and his righteousness and all these things would be added unto you. So before you pray for anything else today, make sure that you pray, "Thy Kingdom come, Thy will be done." Cause that's REAL success...

Pray with me:

Father, I confess that this world's value system is tempting. I sometimes find myself judging people by what they have and judging Your faithfulness to me by what you've blessed me with. Please forgive me. Show me your true riches. Make me a success in Your eyes. In Jesus' Name, Amen.

DAY NINE

Read Luke 1:57-63

Find Your Voice

From the moment you were born, you were being told who to be. Your religion, your race, your political party, etc. People have been telling you how to feel and what to believe and most of us swallowed it whole, even though there's a voice deep inside you saying that's not really who I am. Good news: you're not the only one. Do you know what I've discovered? People who are "different" make "normal" people very nervous. It's been happening since the Bible times. From the moment John the Baptist was born, people were trying to control his destiny. They wanted to silence the uniqueness of his voice. They wanted him to be like his father or someone else they could relate to. He couldn't be different. He couldn't be new. He couldn't hear an authentically different Voice. But the Holy Spirit took care of that. He gave him a different name and a different style. As a matter of fact, by the time we see John again, he's living in the wilderness wearing camel's hair and eating bugs. Yeah. That's real different…But Jesus said that there was no person in history that was greater than John the Baptist. Message: Be yourself. Find your voice and lift it high for the world to hear. Fulfill your destiny or the world will miss it.

Pray with me:

Father I am so thankful that you created me just the way that I am. Please protect me from everyone that would seek to conform me to their image. Even if they are my friends. I thank you for the wonderful destiny you have just for me. In Jesus' Name, Amen.

DAY TEN

Read Genesis 3:1-7

Bondage or Freedom

Have you ever had to use the GPS to go somewhere that you had never been? Let's say D.C. Now imagine you are approaching the D.C. area and the GPS says, "Now you can take 495..." "Or you could take 395...Awwww Shucks. You might wanna take 295! Or get off at this exit and turn left! Or stay on 95North and 495 West and..." Does that sound like a recipe for joy and peace or a recipe for a mental breakdown?! Some of y'all are disturbed just at the thought! But that's exactly what satan does. Satan tried to convince Eve (and us) that "true freedom" is found in having more choices. Don't just listen to Jesus. Try some Islam. Try some Tarot cards. Check out this new funky "worship the earth" thing. He tries to make you feel like you're being "closed minded" when you decide to follow Jesus only. But the truth is that too many choices can paralyze you, not liberate you. There is only one True God. And only one way to the Father and that's through His Son Jesus Christ.

If you're like me, you don't want a GPS that gives you choices while you're driving! You want the GPS that tells me the RIGHT route. Jesus is always the right route.

Pray with me:
Father, satan is always trying to make me feel like I'm missing something. But I thank you that you created my life and you already know the best decisions for me. Please don't let me have to learn the hard way. Let me obey your will the FIRST time. Thank you Daddy. In Jesus's Name, Amen.

DAY ELEVEN

Read Hebrews 4:12

Blind Spots

So I'm driving my dad to Nashville right, and this car is trying to switch lanes. Clearly though, since I am in the lane RIGHT BESIDE him, he won't actually continue his attempt to get over. Wrong.
Several horn beeps and angry looks later, (pray for me) we safely pass this terrible driver! While his poor driving skills angered me in the moment, the truth is that he suffered from a condition that we all have: Blind Spots. He made a life and death decision without being able to see all of the factors and almost paid the ultimate price for it.

And every time you make a decision without consulting the Word of God, you do the same thing.

The Word of God is the only CURE for blind spots.

The Word is a mirror, a Sword, A discerner and a guide. (James 1:23 Eph 6:17, Psalm, 119:105)

Simply put: All human beings have blind spots but the Word does not.

So the next time you are about to make a decision- any decision- make sure that you check your blind spot. Consult the Word of God.

Pray with me:
Father I thank you for the wise counsel that is found in your word. Please give me enough sense to read it.
In Jesus's Name, Amen.

DAY TWELVE:

Read Jonah 4:1-3

I disagree

Do you know why Jonah ended up in the belly of a big fish? He didn't like God's plan.

God told Jonah to go and preach to the Ninevites. But Jonah was a "hater". He literally didn't want to preach to them because he knew they would repent and get saved. And he wanted them to die.

But I'm not really here to talk about Jonah's anointed yet pathological and slightly racist theology... I want to talk about his attitude. God said something he didn't like and his response to God was no. It didn't wind up working out too well for Jonah (disobeying God, that is) and it won't work out for us either.

Let me tell you something that someone should have told you a long time ago, "God loves you. But your opinion does not matter. God's will is final." He is the Master; I am the slave. Period. When God speaks, our only response is "Yes Sir."

Pray with me;

Father I repent for living my life as if your will needed my approval. I am the slave. You are the master. I live to love and serve You. In Jesus's Name, Amen.

DAY THIRTEEN

Read 2 Samuel 11:1-4, 2 Corinthians 12:9-10

Tragic Hero

David was a warrior. He was a conqueror. But it was his ability to "conquer" that allowed him to passionately "conquer" Bathsheba.

Point: Is your greatest strength also your greatest weakness? Is your loving attitude making you gullible? Is your "type A" personality causing you to be a champion at work and a failure with your family? Is your great humility causing self esteem problems? Is your success with crucifying your flesh also causing you to become a bit prideful?

How do we deal with our strengths becoming weaknesses?

By turning our weaknesses into strengths.

Paul basically said, I don't celebrate my victories; I celebrate the God who loves me through my failures. I don't brag about my accomplishments, I brag about the God who uses me in spite of me. I don't focus on myself at all. I focus on Him.

I'm the "tragic"... He's the Hero.

Pray with me:
Father I thank you that you created me with all of my strengths and all of my flaws. Thank you for using me in spite of my flaws. And Please don't let my "strengths" get in Your way.
In Jesus's Name, Amen.

DAY FOURTEEN

Read Ecclesiastes 1:1-9, Ecclesiastes 12: 13-14

Vanity

WORTHLESS!!!! Life is all meaningless and worthless!!! Doesn't exactly sound like the most motivational sermon you've ever heard, does it? But that's exactly what the "world's wisest man" said when he spoke about human existence.

Solomon was rich. He built the greatest kingdom in the world. He had every pleasure imaginable at his fingertips. He had Rubies, diamonds, spices, precious stones, exotic scents, fabrics, servants, armies, chariots, and wives... Lots of wives.

And his conclusion was that it was all "vanity". (Meaningless) Deep, huh? But does Solomon end his story there? Is life just worthless and meaningless? Yes and no. No, life is not meaningless because when we love God and keep His commandments. We find a peace and purpose that we could never did anywhere else. (Ecclesiastes 12:13) But I think the point that Solomon was making (and the point I want you to chew on) is that life IS meaningless; completely meaningless...without God. So if you ever find yourself feeling empty or unfulfilled, it just means that there's not enough God in your life. Because His presence is the only thing that makes life worth living!

Pray with me:

Father I thank you that your love gives me life! You are the source of my strength and the strength of my life. You are my joy, my purpose and my peace. Please help me to remember that today. In Jesus's Name, Amen.

Final Thought: Every pursuit outside of God is vanity. It will never bring lasting happiness…

DAY FIFTEEN

Read Proverbs 26:11

Don't go back

"As a dog returns to his vomit, so a fool returns to his folly."

Did you know that a dog will throw something up and then come back later and lick it? Nasty huh?
I mean REAL nasty!
And that's exactly what you look like to God when you willingly go back into a situation that He delivered you from.

Maybe it was a bad relationship, or an abusive friendship. Maybe it was an addiction or a bad habit or a nasty attitude. Maybe it was unforgiveness or an old lifestyle that you were living before you got saved.

Whatever it is, for God's sake, don't go back!!!

If the dog vomited up the food the first time that means that it didn't agree with him.
If God delivered you the first time, don't take His Grace lightly. The next time might not be so pleasant.

Pray with me:
Father please give me the wisdom and the strength to stay away from what You have delivered me from. In Jesus's Name, Amen.

DAY SIXTEEN

Read Colossians 1:24-29

The Difference

The world needs a Savior....Newsflash: it's not you.
People need to hear the gospel (good news) and experience salvation. They need to see the difference that Jesus Christ makes when He enters your heart. And all of that happens in spite of you. Do you know why true evangelism very seldom takes place? Because we don't really know what makes us different.

It's not your religion. (Adherence to a set of Rules). It's not your style of dress or your moral code or your denomination. It's not the number of spiritual gifts you claim to have or the number of people you have brought to Christ. It's not how much you give to the poor or to the church. It's not how many mission trips you have been on or whether or not you were a Virgin when you got married. The difference is simple: Jesus Christ LIVES inside of you. Evangelism happens when the Love of God shines through you into the heart of an unsaved person.

It's not our job to beat them over the head with doctrine. The scripture says "Christ IN you, the hope of glory." Try to downplay the "you" in you so that the CHRIST in you can be seen!

Pray with me:
Father I thank you that your spirit is more than able to represent Himself. Please don't let my foolish ideas about 'proper evangelism' get in the way of You actually saving souls. I pray this in Jesus's name, Amen!

DAY SEVENTEEN

Read Philippians 4:4-8

Stress

Life will always bring you difficult situations and decisions that have to be made. But did you know that stress was a choice? Let me prove it to you. Have you ever noticed that money problems bother some people but not others? Have you ever worked a job where the boss got on everybody's nerves except the one or two people who knew how to ignore him? Have you ever seen someone with "road rage" ride in a car with someone who couldn't care less about the driver who just cut them off? Of course you have. Because stress is a choice.
"Stress" only occurs when you place a high level of emotional importance on an outcome that is out of your control. If you CHOOSE to meditate on the possibility of a negative outcome in any given situation then you will find yourself stressed. But if you meditate on things that are "pure, lovely and of good report" then you CAN'T be stressed. The word says "He'll keep you in perfect peace if you keep your mind stayed on him".

The choice is yours...

Pray with me:
Father, teach me how to rebuke the demon of stress. I no longer make excuses for stress in my life. I take authority over that demon and speak peace to my own spirit. In Jesus's Name, A-men!

DAY EIGHTEEN

Read Matthew 7:21-27

Practice what you preach

Simple question:
Do your actions line up with what you claim to believe?

Do you believe in tithing?
Do you tithe?

Do you believe that regular church attendance is important?
Do you actually attend church on Sundays and Wednesdays?

Do you believe that unforgiveness is wrong? But you still have it in your heart?

Do you believe that lying, cheating, cursing, and gluttony are wrong?
Do you ever lie, curse, cheat or overeat?

Do you practice what you claim to believe? Jesus said "not everyone who says 'Lord, Lord' will enter into the kingdom. But he who does the will of my Father." It doesn't matter if you can "talk the talk". Jesus said, you gotta walk the walk.

Pray with me:
Father I thank you that your grace covers all of my sin. Now God I ask that my walk match my talk. I pray that everything that I do today would line up with everything that I've learned from your Word. In Jesus's Name, Amen.

DAY NINETEEN

Read Mark 10:17-27

Affluenza

Do you know why the love of money is a root of all kinds of evil? Do you know why money can become the ULTIMATE idol god? One word: Control.

If I have enough money I can make my own decisions and I can ultimately live my life independently of God's rules or standards. For example: Why tithe if I'm already a billionaire? I don't really need Him to open up the floodgates anymore do I?

Why forgive? Why go to work? Why pursue purpose? Why try to help people? Why even pray? Isn't money really the answer to half of our prayers? For example: Do you really need a new job or do you just want more money? Is your spouse really that bad or is your marriage just hard because you're broke?

What about the new car you want? Or the new house? Or the better health insurance or the degree for yourself or the kids? Wouldn't money solve all of those problems???

So who needs God...?

Pray with me:
Father I thank you that you are the sovereign Lord and that you have a plan for my life. Lord I pray that you remove the distraction of money from any of my plans or goals or motives. Let money be my servant and not my master. In Jesus's Name, Amen.

DAY TWENTY

Read Jeremiah 32:36-42

Who is serving Whom?

Question: When it comes to God, are you just looking for someone to answer life's problems or are you looking for relationship?

Case in point: what happens to your relationship with God when He doesn't give you answers to life's problems? Is God JUST "Jireh" to you? Does He only exist to provide for you what you need? Money, peace, answers, pain medication, a spouse, a car? Is God's main purpose in your life to be your heavenly provider? Is your relationship solely based on what God can do for you? Is that the Gospel?

Did Jesus die and rise again so that He could become your heavenly "bell hop"? Your All-Powerful Concierge? Your omnipotent "hook up" man? Or is there more to Relationship with Christ than what He can do for you?

The Children of Israel fell into the trap of thinking that Jehovah existed to serve them. They couldn't fall because "God was on their side"... So, after Jerusalem fell... God promised Jeremiah that He would restore the people. But God spoke of a future where "they will be MY people and I will be their God." I don't think God exists to serve us. I think we exist to love and serve Him.

Pray with me:

Father I repent for insulting you. I have prayed and talked to you as if your only purpose in my life was to satisfy my needs. I'm sorry. Teach me how to love and serve You. In Jesus's Name Amen.

DAY TWENTY-ONE

Read Luke 15:11-24

My Father

My family took a trip to Virginia Beach and my dad paid for everything. Food, travel, hotel... Everything. There was only one stipulation: You had to stay on his agenda.

Now, don't get me wrong, you were free to drive your own car and go wherever you wanted. But if you wanted the gas to be free, you had to ride with him.

You were free to eat wherever you wanted, whenever you wanted. But if you wanted the meal to be free then you had to eat when he ate and at the restaurant he chose.

What's my point?

Just like the prodigal son, A lot of us want the blessings of God but we want to call our own shots. God is willing and able to bless you beyond your wildest dreams but those blessings come with a price: Obedience to His will. God is only obligated to finance HIS WILL. His decisions. His plan. When you move on your own... You're on your own.

Pray with me:
Father I thank you that you are the perfect provider. Father I confess that sometimes I get spoiled and want to disrespect your rules and your plan and do things my way. Please forgive me and give me an obedient heart. In Jesus' Name, Amen.

DAY TWENTY-TWO

Read Hebrews 12:1-11

But did you die?!

In 2009 a comedy was released entitled "The Hangover". There was a little Asian guy (who has become super famous) that had a catch phrase whenever they did something ridiculously dangerous. They would just escape with their lives from some extremely dangerous situation and just as they began to complain, the Asian guy would say, "Yeah, BUT DID YOU DIE????"

It was his way of saying that whatever you're complaining about really wasn't that serious. And in the 12th chapter of Hebrews I can almost hear that little Asian guy's accent when the writer says "you have not yet resisted unto blood..."

In other words, what you're going through may SEEM rough right now but let's keep it in perspective. Don't forget that people have died for being Christians. They were thrown to the lions, burned alive and of course, crucified.

So the next time you feel like jumping on the pity wagon just remember, if you're still alive to tell about it then it can't be that bad! Smile!

Pray with me:
Father I repent for making a big deal out of things that other Christians would laugh at. Thank you that my "trials" are as easy as they are. I rejoice in being able to suffer a "little" for the kingdom! In Jesus's Name, Amen!

DAY TWENTY-THREE

Read Matthew 6:19-21

Packing
I love to travel. But I can't stand packing.

I always have this irrational fear that I'm leaving something.
(And I usually am)
Have you ever packed for a long trip, only to get there and find
that you left a toothbrush or underwear or a belt or deodorant?
What an uncomfortable feeling!

Well, Jesus mentioned packing too. Only He was talking about
eternity. He told us to lay up treasures in heaven where moth and
rust wouldn't corrupt and where thieves would not break through
and steal.
God wants us to spend our time down here focusing on the
things that have heavenly value.

Can you imagine getting to heaven and God saying, "You forgot
something"...?

Think about it...

Pray with me:
Father I thank you that Jesus died for me and packed my
bags for eternity. Please teach me what it means to lay up
treasures in heaven and not just focus on earthly riches.
In Jesus' Name, Amen.

Final Thought: Store up for yourselves treasures in
heaven.

DAY TWENTY-FOUR

Read Psalms 121

Hills

I'm not fond of hills.

I have recently started riding a bike again. (Yes, yes, I know) But the track around my apartment complex is full of hills! And if you have ever ridden a bike up a hill, you know that it is not fun! But as I was riding today I thought, without the hills, this wouldn't be much of a workout. Hills make me pedal harder which in turn makes my muscles bigger and helps me lose more weight. A smooth ride would be much more enjoyable but much less effective.

David said, "I will look to the hills from whence cometh my help. My help cometh from The Lord who made heaven and earth." While I believe that David was referring to God as his help, I also believe that God gave us spiritual hills to climb that help us build the strength that we need to overcome life's other obstacles.

The hills really are our help.

Pray with me;
Father, I thank you for every hill that I've had to climb, both spiritually and physically. Please help me to grow stronger through every obstacle that I overcome and let none of the strength be wasted. In Jesus's Name, Amen.

DAY TWENTY-FIVE

Read Genesis 32:22-32

From Relief to Release

Jacob had been hustling his whole life. He hustled his brother out if his birthright. He hustled his brother AND his father out of the blessing that belonged to the first born. He hustled his uncle Laban out of the best sheep. (He was also hustled BY his uncle and tricked into working 14 years)

But by the time we get to our text Jacob was tired of hustling. He was tired of looking over his shoulder; tired of wondering how he was going to rob Peter to pay Paul; tired of using his wits to survive. Jacob was a desperate man. He thought his brother was coming to kill him. Then all of a sudden an angel of The Lord wrestles with him. Jacob must have been a pretty good wrestler because the bible said that the angel couldn't prevail. So the angel dislocated Jacob's hip. The pain must have been excruciating. But Jacob refused to let go.

Do you know what Jacob was saying? "I know that this situation is painful but it can't hurt worse than my life already does. I would love to get *relief* from this pain but not as much as I want to get *released* from the bondage I have lived with for my entire life. So if I have to deal with some temporary pain now, I don't mind because I want a permanent deliverance." We should all be like Jacob. Or should I say "Israel"...

Pray with me:
Father, I am no longer praying for relief. I don't want the quick fix. I don't want you to numb the pain. I am praying that you would reveal the SOURCE of the pain and heal me completely. No matter how painful it is. I want to be truly free. In Jesus's Name, Amen!

DAY TWENTY-SIX

Read Romans 8:28

Christian Regret?

Maybe it was a bad relationship that you regret starting. Maybe it was a good relationship that you regret ending. Maybe it was a decision that you made that you wish you could change. A job you wish you had applied for... A financial decision that ended badly. Maybe you got pregnant "too soon"... Perhaps you regret getting married or not getting married. Or missing a golden opportunity. Whatever the issue is, a lot of people live with regret. They tell themselves that if I had just done this or not done that, then my life would be better now.

Can I tell you a secret? It's a lie. Not only is it a lie but it really exposes a lack of faith in God. Romans 8:28 says all things work together for good. Jeremiah 29:11 says "I know the plans that I have for you".

Ephesians 1:11 says that God works "all things according to the counsel of His own will".

Regret not only causes undue stress and sadness (because you can't go back) but it also hinders your faith that God is somehow creating a happy ending.

So make this declaration with me today:

Everything that happened to me is going to work out for good! I have nothing to regret because God said, "It's ALL GOOD!"

Pray with me:
Father I thank you that I don't have to live with regret. You have amazing plans for me and they were already finished before I was born. Thank you for choosing me for this awesome destiny! In Jesus's Name, Amen.

DAY TWENTY-SEVEN

Read Luke 4:1-13

Jesus Christ Superstar

Have you noticed that nowadays it's hard to tell who the "star" is at church? I mean, are we celebrating Jesus or the pastor? Are we spreading His message or theirs? And exactly whose name are we trying to make great? There seems to be a lot of confusion in the church today. Ministers are "branding" themselves instead of making Jesus famous. But this temptation for spiritual leaders didn't start with "Mega Church" pastors. Over 2,000 years ago satan tried to tempt Jesus in the same way. First he tried His flesh with physical hunger. Then he tested His loyalty by offering Him the praises of men. But lastly, when He couldn't get Jesus to do any of that, He tried the religious route. "Make a big spectacle of yourself, throw yourself down and let God catch you! You'll be famous then!"

"Yeah. No. How about I just preach and teach and heal and let the Father be famous?"

Satan is using the same tricks on you and I today. Will it be your physical desires? Or will it be the ungodly culture that gets you? What about the desire to be great? Will it be pride that opens the door for satan to enter?

Pray about it... With me...
Father we thank you that you always give us a way of escape when temptation comes. God, show us when we think we're following You but we're really being tricked by the enemy. Use us for Your glory. And don't let it be the other way around. In Jesus's Name, Amen.

DAY TWENTY-EIGHT

Read Exodus 15:32-26

Believe in Your Healing

Have you ever wondered why we don't see the healings that we read about in the bible?

Lame people waking, blind people seeing, deaf people hearing?

Has God changed?

Has He run out of power? Is He somehow different now? Maybe He just wants us to be sick.

No brothers and sisters, none of those things are true. God is still "Jehovah Rapha", the God that heals us. And in order for us to start seeing the healing, we must first believe that God is not only able but willing to heal us.

Start by making this simple affirmation with me:
"God wants me to be healed."

Pray with me:
Father, I thank You for Your healing power. Heal me from every sickness and disease that is plaguing my body. And then God, heal me from every disease that is attacking my mind and my spirit. I Thank you that it is Your desire to heal me. In Jesus' Name, Amen.

DAY TWENTY-NINE

Read 1 Samuel 8:1-7

Be careful what you ask for

How many times have you prayed for a relationship only to turn around and pray for God to get you out of it?

How many times have you prayed for a new job, only to have to turn around and ask God for ANOTHER new job? What if we stopped asking God for stuff and trusted that He already has the best plan for our lives...?

The children of Israel asked for a King so they could be like other nations. And that's exactly what they got. And things got worse and worse for them...

The next time you find yourself begging for something that God doesn't seem to want to give you,
Stop.

Pray with me:
Father I thank you for your perfect will. PLEASE don't give me anything that will hurt me. Even if I ask for it.
Show me the "good and perfect gifts" that you have already given me. In Jesus' Name, Amen.

DAY THIRTY

Read Ecclesiastes 3: 1-8; John 12:24

Let's get 'Tore Up'!

How do you build muscle?
You have to tear the old muscle and the new muscle rebuilds itself on top of the old.

How do you build a new building? You have to tear up the ground and lay a foundation before you do anything else. You must go DOWN before you can come up.

How do you make a cake? You start by breaking an egg.

How do you create a butterfly? You destroy a caterpillar.

What am I saying? I'm saying that God always tears something up when he's getting ready to build something greater. When God gets ready to elevate you to the next level in your life, He often destroys the things that were keeping you bound. Even if you liked those things. Especially if you liked those things.

In this season, pay attention to what God is destroying. And stay out of His way...

Pray with me:
Father I thank you for your perfect plan in my life. God I confess that it looks crazy sometimes but I know your thoughts are higher than my thoughts. Father, I give you permission to tear up everything that has outlasted its usefulness in my life and usher me into my next level. In Jesus' Name, Amen!

Excerpt from Joseph Pridgen's newest book :

"The Power of NOW!!!"

Get this in your spirit: You are already blessed. Already filled. Already destined for greatness.

Whenever an architect gets ready to build a building, where do you think they start? With the first floor? The basement? What about the foundation? Nope, none of the above. They don't start with digging the hole, clearing the space or importing the dirt either. They start with a blueprint. That's right. Before one bulldozer is cranked, before one slab of concrete is poured and before one sweaty construction worker starts earning a paycheck, the building is already finished in the mind of the architect. Every brick, every ounce of material, every measurement and every hour of manpower has already been meticulously planned and accounted for. In fact, the very fact that you see builders working is proof that the design is not only finished but perfect.

The bible says before you were in your mother's womb God knew you and appointed you to be a prophet to the nations. My friend, God is the Master Architect. Before you were ever born He "finished" you. He knew every mistake and every masterpiece that you would ever make. And before you were ever born, he stepped back and said, "It's good." "For I know the plans that I have for you; Plans to prosper you and not to harm you, to give you a future and a hope." The steps of a good man are ordered by the Lord and He delights in his way.

As I previously stated, the bible declares that you were fearfully and wonderfully made. Why is that important? Because that means you don't have to work to *become* something. You don't have to create intelligence or gifting or a passion for some sort of work. The only thing that you have to do is "dis-cover" who God already created you to be. All you have to do is learn what makes you tick and what ticks you off. When you discover the voice inside you that only you can hear, your only job is to follow it like your life depends on it. Because it does.

About the Author

Joseph B. O. Pridgen is an anointed Pastor, Teacher, Life Coach, Singer/Songwriter, Workshop Facilitator and Soon to be Best Selling Author. He holds a Master's of Divinity Degree from Payne Theological Seminary. He has been preaching the gospel for over 15 years and he has been pastoring for the last 9 years. He recently added "church planter" to his resume when he founded "The POWER Church", in February of 2014. He lives in North Carolina with his wife Kenya Pridgen.

For Booking information or to order more copies please visit our website: www.josephpridgen.com or call @ 919-798-0273.

Made in the USA
San Bernardino, CA
24 June 2016